How to create a Trade Mark, Protect it and build your Brand

by Liam M. Birkett

Copyright 2014 © Liam M. Birkett

www.LiamMBirkett.com

D0774628

Relevant internationally

The general principles of intellectual property rights are similar internationally. This is because I P law has been largely been harmonised, for example in the EU. (There will always be exceptions to the general rule in some jurisdictions.)

Search of Trade Mark Registers

It is essential that, before using a new brand identity, a search is made of the target markets (be that Ireland, the UK, the EU or further afield) to ensure that it does not infringe the rights of others. Expert advice, such as that of a Trade Mark Attorney, is advisable because what appears to be clear to the untrained eye may, in fact, conceal a sustainable objection from a rival.

Self-search

From the outset, at no cost to yourself, you can search the various trade mark offices to discover any direct hits that show that your intended mark is already registered.

The registration process

Trade marks are generally registered on a country-by country basis. However, the Community Trade Mark enables the brand owner, by means of a single CTM filing, to register his or her trade mark across the entire territory of the EU.

IMPORTANT - Study pages 60/61/62 in this book

Links to some free international search facilities:

Ireland   http://www.patentsoffice.ie
UK   http://www.ipo.gov.uk/

EU (all 28 member states)
https://www.tmdn.org/tmview/welcome

This website also includes a free online database for other countries which are outside the EU such as the United States, Russia, Turkey, and Korea. It provides links to other search databases such as ASEAN TMVIEW which facilitates search in a number of Asian countries including Malaysia, Singapore, and Thailand.

United States   http://tmsearch.uspto.gov

Canada   http://www.cipo.ic.gc.ca/tm

Australia   http://pericles.ipaustralia.gov.au/atmoss/falcon.application_start

Caution
These databases are a great tool for trade mark searching. Without professional assistance, they should not be regarded as being other than a preliminary indication as to whether a desired trade mark is available for use or registration in a given country.

Contents

HOW TO CREATE YOUR TRADE MARK, PROTECT IT AND BUILD YOUR BRAND

Learn how to go about devising your trade mark. The essential steps to ensure that you can use, register and protect it. Read how easy it is to add value to your brand and use branding to get free publicity.

Because I have "been there, done that" you are assured that this is not an academic lesson.
I will save you time, money and heartache by telling you what to do and what to avoid. You will benefit from knowing the direct route to creating a strong branding. All that you will read in this book is fully supported with a wide range of examples from real life experiences that illustrate each point.

SECTION OVERVIEW

CHAPTER 1

In this section you will learn how to go about creating a trade mark. The misconceptions regarding a limited liability company name. You will see that it does not have the same scope, or benefits, of a registered trade mark.

Similarly, a domain name registration also has limitations. Its shortcomings should be fully understood and appreciated.

A Business Name Registration (a stipulation that relates only to the Republic of Ireland) does not give you permission to use that name in trade. Nor does it bestow exclusivity on that name.

You will appreciate how all of this impacts on you when you begin the task of creating your own brand.

CHAPTER 2

In this section are more examples that highlight the shortcomings of a limited liability company name and business name registration as compared to the benefits of a registered trade mark.

The value of a domain name is explored along with its vulnerability and the need to take further steps to protect its long term rights.

All this builds on what has gone before and expands your knowledge base.

CHAPTER 3

On these pages we go through all of the steps that are required to check out the branding you aim to use and how to secure the exclusivity you want.

CHAPTER 4

This section explains all about the Community Trade Mark. This facility allows you, with just application, to seek protection of your mark in all 28 (as of now) member states of the EU.

CHAPTER 5

We now concentrate on the creative process of devising a trade mark for the goods or service you wish to brand and protect.   In so doing you are now more fully armed with all that you have learned from the previous sections.

You know that to obtain registration of your new branding you have to comply with the stipulations itemised on those earlier pages.   With these in mind you start to work on the daunting task of being truly creative.

CHAPTER 6

On these pages are examples of how, by creating a clever trade mark, the attention of the consumer was immediately captured. It was also the ideal platform for widespread media coverage. These will act as a guide, and perhaps an inspiration, for you when you undertake the task of trade mark creation.

CHAPTER 7

Beginning below on this page is an article that was part of a series. It refers to a seminar I delivered to a large audience of business people. I have added bold statements throughout the article to emphasise each of the various forms trade mark registration can take. It will also assist you when revisiting the subject and working on your own project. By using them you will add greatly to the recognition and memorability of what it is you are marketing.

CHAPTER 8

There is another side to the branding story of which you should be aware. I referred to it in another article I penned some time back. Here are extensive details of costly issues to be avoided and matters to be mindful of in respect of your business.

CHAPTER 9

Here is a selection of very interesting stories related to very well-known brands with international reputations. Mistakes made and some which were overcome.

CHAPTER 10

Some very important information regarding Domain addresses. The pros and cons associated with them and the essential understanding you should have of their value and use.

CHAPTER 11

How many of the most recognised trade marks came into being

CHAPTER 12

Recap on what you have learned and how this assists you in reaching your objectives

PROFILE

Liam Birkett is changing the way many people and firms do business. No matter the size of firm or the budget one has, he brings a refreshing enthusiasm, insight and expertise that creates and turns business ideas into reality.

Liam's career began in office management then evolved into sales and marketing. He was involved in the launch of Mace and VG group in Ireland. His experience extended into wholesale, retail, cash & carry, and consultancy on a national and international basis before moving to O'Kennedy Brindley Advertising (later to become Saatchi & Saatchi).

With colleagues from the advertising agency, he founded Bernardini, Birkett & Gardner Ltd, a design & marketing consultancy which, for more than 20 years was responsible for corporate identities and many marketing initiatives for blue chip companies as well as SMEs. This embraced branding as well as graphic and packaging projects for a long list of high profile clients. He is a past president of the Society of Designers in Ireland.

His unique skill is to see matters from a design, marketing and sales perspective. Couple this with a comprehensive understanding of Intellectual property to generate a unique way of looking at existing or new business opportunities.

He shows how dangers can be avoided, businesses can be improved, find new angles for old business, and dream up new lines. Moreover, he can demonstrate how all this can be utilised to obtain publicity for the resulting business, product or service. Again, these claims are based on results he himself has achieved.

He fits into the "commercialisation" slot for whatever business or service, in whatever sector, is in need of support. Many people have good ideas, products or services but do not have the ability to commercialise them and, in the absence of a worthwhile promotional fund, cannot obtain essential media exposure. Liam can! Being the creator of brands and an inventor himself, he has "been there, done that" on all counts.

One such commission was for O'Darby Irish Cream liqueur, leading to being appointed marketing, and then managing, director of the company. He launched the product on 17 world markets overseeing its development and ultimate sale to the Bacardi Corporation. He has marketed in half the states of the United States and also worked for the People's Republic of China advising companies on how to develop products for the West and market them over here.

Because of his depth of knowledge in Intellectual Property (IP), acquired through progressing branding and patents on behalf of clients and himself, he was asked by the largest IP law firm on the island, to market that firm. The challenge was to make the subject matter interesting, attractive, relevant and meaningful to everyone!

For seven years he was an intellectual property consultant with the firm recording outstanding results far exceeding everyone's expectations. During this period he was regularly on radio, TV and in newspapers and magazines. He is sought out as a pundit on such matters. He has been repeatedly asked back to speak to university classes, business groups and professional bodies both national and international.

This same collection of attributes he employs for his clients bringing into existence and publicising their products and services. He is regularly chosen to deliver workshops, seminars, clinics and assist client groups and businesses to create new ventures and instil new life into going concerns.

He was chosen by the European Commission to deliver his expertise to SMEs in entrant countries to the EU and by the EU Scientific Committee to deliver a paper on IP and marketing to an international workshop on *Personalised Health: The Integration of Innovative Sensing, Textile, Information & Communication Technologies* - the synergies between advanced textiles, sensors, nanotechnology and ICT).

He is a Consultant Expert to the European Commission Framework Programme.

INTRODUCTION

Easy to understand

This book was written as a response to many requests made to me over my years associated with devising trademarks, creating brands and promoting the benefits of intellectual property. The call came from clients, from readers of my articles, listeners to my radio contributions and especially from the many attendees at my seminars.

Entertaining and accessible

All these groups told me repeatedly that they wanted a more detailed record of what I had said or written. Time and again, people came to me saying that my approach was entertaining, easy to understand and that my delivery makes the subject matter accessible to everyone.

Relevant internationally

The general principles of intellectual property rights are similar internationally. This is because I P law has largely been harmonised, for example in the EU. (There will always be exceptions to the general rule in some jurisdictions.) Because many of my talks and seminars are given in Ireland, the content frequently cites Irish examples. Nevertheless these examples are relevant to international situations.

HOW TO CREATE A TRADE MARK, PROTECT IT AND BUILD YOUR BRAND

In this book you will learn the intricate process to follow in the creation of your trade mark and the building of your brand. It shows you how you can bring your big idea to life. You have been dreaming of creating a brand that will influence people's lives, nationally or internationally. This shows you how to achieve your aims.

TRADE MARK/BRAND

These terms are constantly used interchangeably. In fact they have different meanings. A company's brand, or branding, refers to the overall impression created and associated with the company's image, its trade marks, designs, reputation and status.

The APPLE and ROLLS ROYCE brands invoke a great deal more about the businesses in the mind of the consumer than their trade marks alone.

Make your business stand out

In the following pages you will read how to create a suitable trade mark (and build a brand) for the goods or service you intend to market. One that will make them jump off the shelves. You want to create winners and you want to protect them. This shows you how to do just that.

WHAT TO USE

You will learn the essential characteristics that should be part of the mark you devise. Each step to take in the process is explained to ensure that your mark can be legally used and registered in your target markets. You then enjoy exclusivity.

WHAT TO AVOID

There are very many types of word to be avoided which, to the uninitiated, may appear attractive and suitable.

Their unacceptability and/or shortcomings are highlighted. You will know the shortcuts to success.

MORE STRENGTH

The chosen branding can be further embellished by employing a wide range of additional forms of trade mark – logotypes, symbols, slogans, shapes, smells and more. These are set out in great detail.

REAL LIFE EXAMPLES

All of the above is fully supported with a wide range of examples from real life experiences that illustrate each point. Because I have "been there, done that" you are assured that this is not an academic lesson.

I will save you time, money and heartache by telling you what to avoid. You will benefit from knowing the direct route to creating a strong branding.

Repeat and remember

No apology is made for the repetition of the most important elements. These are included at each stage to help you remember what you need to know when creating your trade mark and building your brand.

EASY ACCESS
These points facilitate you to dip in and out of the pages from time to time when you want to check out relevant facts and guidelines.

HERE ARE THE BENEFITS TO YOU
- You will learn how to devise a trade mark the essential steps to ensure that you can use the mark
- How to register and protect it
- Multiple types of trade marks
- The misconceptions regarding company names
- Errors relating to domain names
- How to use branding to get free publicity
- How to add value to your brand
- A strategy to follow for expansion
- Practical examples of trade marks in use

CHAPTER 1 - TRADE MARKS AND MISCONCEPTIONS

In this section you will learn how to go about creating a trade mark. The misconceptions regarding a company name. You will see that it does not have the same scope, or benefits, of a registered trade mark.

Similarly, a domain name registration also has limitations. Its shortcomings should be fully understood and appreciated.

A Business Name Registration (a stipulation that relates only to the Republic of Ireland) does not give you permission to use that name in trade. Nor does it bestow exclusivity on that name.

You will appreciate how all of this impacts on you when you begin the task of creating your own brand.

CREATING A TRADE MARK

Over a great many years I have worked for clients developing new trade marks for them, sometimes in conjunction with my brilliant partner, Walter Bernardini. This became all the more challenging for me as my knowledge extended into knowing more about the legal stipulations and the requirements to obtain trade mark registration.

LOGIC AND PROCESS

During all this time I have been asked constantly where the inspiration comes from in creating a trade mark. In this book I want to pass on to you the logic and process used. At the same time I will acquaint you with the fundamentals in relation to the trade mark registration process.

USE AND REGISTRATION

It is one thing to come up with a clever mark but it is an entirely different challenge to create one that can be legally used and protected. You need to ensure that you will not infringe the existing rights of others. That is, that someone else does not have an identical or confusingly similar trade mark, for the same goods or services, as you intend to use. If the way is clear then your suggested mark is capable of registration as a trade mark in the class of goods or services you wish to cover, in your targeted countries. When granted, you can then enjoy exclusive rights to its use.

DEFINITION OF A TRADE MARK

The following are the essential points relating to the creation of a trade mark. The legal definition given is as follows: "Any sign capable of being represented graphically which is capable of distinguishing goods or services of one undertaking from those of other undertakings." A trade mark acts as an indication of origin and level of quality and reliability. A Rolls Royce car comes from a specific company and will be associated with a high level of quality.

FORMS OF TRADE MARK

These include, among lots of others, words, symbols, logotypes, letters, numerals, colours, shapes of goods or their packaging, sounds, smells and slogans.

LIMITATIONS

Because trade mark registration bestows exclusive use in the market in which it is registered there are limitations as to what can be registered. (But it is possible to have the same trade mark for completely different goods, for example POLO for a car (VW POLO) and for confectionery (POLO mints).

ABSOLUTE AND RELATIVE

Refusal can be on 1. *Absolute* grounds, that is, the Official Examiner (the official in the Patents Office responsible for adjudicating on trade marks) rules the mark to be descriptive or otherwise lacking in distinctiveness and 2. *Relative* grounds, that is, it infringes earlier rights.

BEST TO AVOID

One should avoid personal names (Jones, Harry's) because a person can honestly attach their own name to their products or services; geographic names (London, Florida) again, if that is where they originate then the name of the location can be used by others; descriptive trade marks (Fresh, Cool) will be considered descriptive of their characteristics; laudatory terms (Smooth, Awesome) may be judged to be descriptive, deceptive or misleading and be difficult to register or will prove to be problematic at some point in their use.

ANOTHER FORM OF PROTECTION

While registration is the best and strongest way to protect your trade mark, certain aspects of branding may be protected by other means even in the absence of (or perhaps pending) trade mark registration.

COPYRIGHT

One of these is copyright. Copyright can provide protection for any original literary, dramatic, musical or artistic work (and others not covered in this book).

LOGOTYPES

For example, copyright protection may apply to some brand elements. Probably the most obvious of these is a logotype. That is the distinctive way in which a trade mark is designed. A classic example of this is the famous Coca Cola logo. Such an element may be protected because it can be judged to be an original artistic work.

SLOGANS AND TAGLINES

However, other brand aspects may also enjoy copyright protection, such as musical jingles (if it is an original musical work). So too, potentially, can a slogan or tagline (it being considered as an original literary work).

AUTOMATIC, INTERNATIONAL AND FREE

Copyright arises automatically upon creation of a protectable work. As a result, it is free and does not need to be registered and the protection extends internationally. That said, it is important to recognise that copyright only protects against actual copying. In many cases this means that it may be difficult and expensive to prove that a competitor has copied your copyrighted brand features.

PROVE ITS EXISTENCE

Moreover, because copyright is not registered, in the event of a dispute, it is necessary to prove both that copyright subsists (that means it exists) in the infringed mark and that you can demonstrate ownership of the protected matter.

LIFE PLUS 70 YEARS

Most businesses are more concerned with the present and near future rather than the long term. However, it is worth noting that, in most instances, copyright expires 70 years after the demise of the author of the copyrighted work.

TRADE MARKS CAN BE PROTECTED FOREVER

In contrast, a registered trade mark can be protected in perpetuity if it is put to proper use and is renewed every ten years.

LIMITATION/CHALLENGES

In summary then, logos and possibly also other brand elements may automatically enjoy some level of protection under copyright even if those features are not the subject of trade mark registration. However, the limitations of, and challenges in enforcing copyright mean that it is almost always advisable to register your trade marks rather than merely relying on copyright protection.

THE CREATIVE PROCESS

Taking all of the above into consideration this book elaborates on the creative process itself and how, in my personal experience, I go about creating suitable marks.

It is, of course, a personal method but one which will facilitate you to follow the same route or inspire you to find your own way to meeting the challenge.

BUT FIRST

However, before exposing myself, so to speak, let's set you a task. You come up with some answers to a trade mark test I set. Refer back to what you have already read.

Take in what is needed, that which could be grounds for refusal of a trade mark and that which is to be avoided. This exercise will refresh your memory and arm you for the test.

To whet your appetite and test your capabilities in this area here are a few challenges with which to wrestle.

1. A funky new bag, specially designed to carry a laptop computer, must have a catchy, memorable trade mark. An overall trade mark for a unique range of sandwiches as well as trade marks for some of the sandwiches on offer.
2. You are tasked with the job of coming up with a suitable trade mark for a new design of kennel for dogs.

3. A leading ladies fashion design house requires a distinctive trade mark that highlights the different colours as the seasons change.

4. For the kiddies market a trade mark for an innovative sweet product.

5. Fashion jewellery whose trade mark will exclude expense and exclusivity.

6. A trade mark for a fruit and vegetable company.

7. A selection of sea food products needs a trade mark that relates to that industry.

Later in this book you will read about the trade marks that were devised for all of the above and the logic behind their creation.

HERE'S HOW I GO ABOUT THE TASK

Although it is possible to select a word, or words, that have no reference to the goods or services to be trade marked, I prefer the covert reference. I do this for a number of reasons. They are all aimed at assisting the target customer to remember what is on offer and to facilitate promotional activity. This has many benefits in that it often offers a great deal of free publicity potential. If something is quirky it captures buyers and media attention.

SOME EXAMPLES

So let's take a few examples. Some of these were registered as trade marks, others are for hypothetical products or services but illustrate the creative process that goes into their creation and the reasoning behind them.

CARRIER CASE

Task 1: A funky new bag is being specially designed to carry a laptop computer.

The target market is young people. My mind starts to analyse the words computer and laptop. I avoid any use of a word containing "compu", or the like, because the marketplace is full of such combinations. I would have little or no hope of gaining exclusivity for a trade mark built around those letters.

AVOID GENERIC WORDS

Then I consider laptop. Again, this is a generic word that refers to any make of laptop from any manufacturer. So no hope there for the bag in question. A laptop bag is a laptop bag and any rival would be at liberty to refer to their version in the same way.

LOOK FOR A COVERT REFERENCE

Then my mind jumped to a lateral approach. I decided on a word that had a covert, or hidden, reference to the product's use.

DANCER

"Dancer" now there was a word that could be registered as a trade mark. One that is suited to the target market. Easy to remember. Unlikely to meet with any objection from the official examiner at the Patents office as it has no direct reference to the goods to which it will be applied.

HIDDEN MEANING

You will agree with all so far but perhaps wonder why choose the word "Dancer"? Then consider that which will be put inside the bag that carries that trade mark. A laptop. Therefore, a laptop - dancer. Now it takes on a whole new significance and is ideally suited for the job. The targeted consumer will probably be familiar with the term Lap Dancer that well known form of late night entertainment. They will also be aware of laptops and can easily make the connection with the chosen trade mark.

ANOTHER EXAMPLE

Task 2: Come up with an overall trade mark for a unique range of sandwiches as well as trade marks for some of the sandwiches on offer

SANDWICHES

The brief was to come up with a new range of sandwiches that would capture the public's imagination and have trade marks in keeping with the ethos of the product.

BUT REALLY INNOVATIVE

These would be no ordinary sandwiches. They would be "Exotic sandwiches with erotic fillings". What was desirable was a trade mark that sat comfortably on such a bold claim.

EXOTIC PASSION

So you think, what do the words exotic and erotic conjure up in the mind? A trade mark that links in easily into the promise suggested by the slogan is PASSION. Add-ons, such as "Did you get your ration of PASSION today? "Exotic sandwiches with erotic fillings", suggest themselves as ideal jingles for advertising and promotional purposes.

INDIVIDUALITY

To accompany this trade mark and to identify individual sandwiches in the range, equally appropriate marks, in the same vein, are a must.

And so BIG HUG, LOVE BITE and FRENCH KISS
were born.

You can readily appreciate the sales and marketing
potential this stable of marks has to the trade, consumer
and advertising people alike.

ANOTHER EXAMPLE

Concocted word

Here is another mental approach used to fill a slightly
unusual brief. It relates to an invention which must have
a trade mark. The product in question is a jigsaw with a
very original, and seemingly senseless, feature.

The word we devised is newly minted one from our
imagination - UDRA. It is likely to be pronounced UD,
as in hood and RA, as in ra, ra, ra. Therefore there is no
obvious barrier to it being accepted as a trade mark for a
board game.

Jigsaw

The innovative product is a jigsaw with this surprising feature - there is no picture on it. It is blank. This allows the user to draw his or her own graphics on its surface using the felt tip pens which are supplied.

Hidden meaning

But let's examine the word mark more closely. What appears to be a purely concocted word has a hidden logic to its creation. The aim was to have a seemingly innocuous title, thus facilitating registration, yet having a covert reasoning in its selection.

Exposed

If pronounced with a different emphasis, UDRA becomes YOU DRAW. Then a "you draw" jigsaw title explains exactly what the product is about!

Another example

Animal logic

A new product is about to be launched. It is a safety device that is placed around the neck of a particular animal, a bull. These creatures can, at times, suddenly turn nasty and attack a farmer. The new device is activated via a hand-held zapper and delivers sufficient electric shock to momentarily incapacitate the animal.

Other business sector

To come up with a trade mark the mind is searched to find a word that conveys the benefit of the new product. What if we could chose a word that means something entirely different when used in another business sector but is spot-on for what is needed here?

Automotive

By thinking about all of the words associated with causing the animal to stumble, falter, stall, be dazed and the like, we found what we were after. Doze.
Add that to the species in question and it combined to be a word used almost exclusively in the automotive industry. Ideal, it fitted the bill exactly. BULLDOZER.

Another example

A good mixer

A client had developed a cream liqueur product. It had a
secret formulation that allowed it to be successfully
mixed with acidic drinks such as colas and fruit juices.
Rival cream liqueurs could not be so mixed.

High profile

To promote the client's liqueur in the United States it
was decided to make the most of this USP (unique
selling proposition). And so a number of cocktails were
formulated and required to be trade marked. Let's take
just one of these to show how exclusive trade mark
rights can be mobilised to, not only protect the mark, but
also be a high profile promotional tool.

Any time

When the cream liqueur was mixed with orange juice it was christened "Top of the morning" and we had the Americans drinking our liqueur as a breakfast treat as well as at all other times.

"Top of the morning" is an expression used as a form of welcome, it is jovial and is probably uniquely associated with the Irish. As it has no direct reference to liqueurs, or any drink for that matter, it makes a perfect trade mark.

ANOTHER EXAMPLE

Fashion House

One particular company manufactured clothes for children. The trade mark it used identified them directly with that age group. However, the executives learned that many of the garments they sold appealed to smaller sized women who were purchasing them for themselves. An obvious shortcoming, and limitation to the garments sales potential, was the reluctance of some women to be seen buying and/or wearing an obvious child's brand.

Appeal to both

For this reason the challenge was to devise a trade mark that would sit happily on a range that could be worn without embarrassment to young and mature alike.

Upper class

The creative process began by seeking a word that had a prestige ring about it. One that would appeal to both age groups. A trade mark which evoked upper class fashion without claiming to be haute couture. A label that was easily remembered for what it stood for and would have a long life.

Fairy tale

By mentally delving in to children's likes and dislikes a well know fairy tale came to mind. This seemed most apt as it involved a ball gown and a young person's desire to be acceptably dressed. In that way the trade mark CINDERELLA was created. It was augmented by coining a slogan "Clothes fit for a princess".

A fitting slogan

The new mark was equally attractive to a young person and to the more mature female of petite stature. Each category was very happy to wear outfits from the CINDERELLA range. The slogan too added allure and value to the outfits, with the inclusion of the word "fit" having a double meaning. Not only were the clothes suitable for a princess, they were the right fit for people of a certain size.

Another example

Fun bun

This time we promote all the ways you can enjoy a BUNDY, (a trade marked hamburger bun) and to do this we looked to the creative fillings you could use. In so doing we added credence with the slogan that went with the product "More fun than a bun".

Kid appeal

To appeal to the end user, mainly young children, the following registerable titles were created. The first involved fillings made up of apples, oranges and nuts. This was called TARZAN. Another made use of any leftovers such as pieces of meat, beans, diced vegetables and was known as a UFO. Fish fingers topped off with tomato ketchup and/or mayonnaise gave us JAWS.

The unusual

One that had huge appeal, because it was a most unlikely filling, involved putting lengths of chocolate flake side by side to resemble timber logs. And so the popular LUMBERJACK came to be. Now you would not think to put a chocolate flake into a hamburger bun but you could into a BUNDY because it's *more fun than a bun!*

Perfect match

Here you can see how each trade mark fits in nicely with the elements that make up the individual offerings. The names reflect the ingredients in every case and they have great attraction for the target market.

Promotion

By utilising this logic not only is the need for identifying the offerings served, it also assists in the advertising and promotional activities that ensue.

Another example

Control

This relates to an innovative drug product that could control the amount of lipids in the body. Too many of these can be harmful to one's health.

Highlight

What was needed was a name that not only referred to the condition but also highlighted the capability of the product to control the condition. To this end what was required would ideally combine the name by which the element was known and the benefit this particular drug had in its suppression.

Double answer

The solution was found by, in addition to devising the word itself, adding in a visual element that clearly indicated a reduction in the danger associated with the complaint.

Three, two, one

The new word was LIPIDAMIN. You will notice in contains the letter "I" three times. By using three dots over the first "I", two over the second and only one over the third, the association of reduction was achieved.

Reduced

The trade mark itself is composed of the word Lipid with the addition of min which is a truncated version of the word "minimise"

Another example

A range of sports attire suitable for all sorts of activity was in need of a trade mark that would single it out as being what was needed for success.

Winner alright

One thinks of that which all would-be winners aspire to in pursuit of their goal. In the great majority the result is determined by one thing alone, the score. And so SCORE made an ideal choice and fulfilled the brief.

It is important for the reader to appreciate the full scope of what is required for branding to do the ideal job. This is all the more significant given the emphasis now placed on the value of memorable web addresses.

Web addresses

In some instances, it may be possible, and indeed, desirable, to have the product or service trade mark and the web address, the same. This puts greater demands on the creative process but, if achieved, can add greatly to the marketing possibilities of the product or service. It can also hugely increase the subsequent value of the brand.

Company name

There will also be times when the chosen trade mark can be used across the full gambit of company name, web address and for the product or service itself. This makes it so easy for the consumer who will easily know how to make a purchase, make contact and have any interaction they desire.

Covering the options

Of course there are times when the company name is already established and the task is to brand a new offering from the company. This book sets out to cover all of the possible permutations that the marketer may be faced with when promoting a business initiative.

Ltd. com .ie BNR

There is a misconception that having a company name or a Business Name Registration (a facility that only exists in the Republic of Ireland) or a domain name registration allows use of that name and provides trade mark protection. Not so!

Exclusive registration

The main and simplest way to obtain exclusive rights to, and protect, the name under which you wish to trade is by way of trade mark registration.

Limited Liability Company

A limited liability company is a separate entity whereby your personal situation can be protected should a venture fail and only the paid up capital of the company is at risk. There are exceptions to this rule, if you have traded fraudulently or have provided personal guarantees.

Not trade mark use

However, having a company name does not automatically give you the right to use that name in trade (i.e. use it as a trade mark) nor does it protect it.

Companies Registration Office

It is possible to obtain a name for a company, and this can be accepted by the Government's Companies Registration Office, but that still does not mean that it can be used for trading purposes.

Web address

Similar to the situation regarding company names, securing a web address has its limitations too. The name you register as a domain name does not bestow permission to use that name in trade nor does it protect it.

As was stated earlier "to obtain exclusive rights to, and protect, the name under which you wish to trade is by way of trade mark registration."

Ideal scenario

An example of all of the above is as follows:
The client has chosen the name TRIDENT as their brand. Ideally, the best case scenario would be if they could secure a trade mark registration of TRIDENT, a domain name registration such as trident.com and/or a national version like .trident.co.uk and, if they decide to trade by means of a company, to do so under the name Trident Ltd.

You are now alert to the misconceptions regarding a company name. You understand that it does not have the same scope, or benefits, of a registered trade mark. More about this later in the book.

You are aware that a domain name registration also has limitations. You have learnt of shortcomings and understand and appreciate them.

You are alert to the fact that a Business Name Registration does not give you permission to use that name in trade. Nor does it bestow exclusivity on that name.

You now appreciate how all of this impacts on your thought process when you begin the task of creating your own brand.

CHAPTER 2– YOU LEARN THE BENEFITS OF A TRADE MARK

On the following pages are more examples that highlight the shortcomings of a company name and business name registration as compared to the benefits of a registered trade mark.

The value of a domain name is explored along with its vulnerability and the need to take further steps to protect its long term rights.

All this builds on what has gone before and expands your knowledge base.

An example

One could have a company called, for instance, Zodiac Goods Ltd. However, if it started selling automobile related goods or services, under that name, is likely to get sustainable objections from the Ford car company if it feels that the use of *Zodiac* infringes a trade mark registrations it holds.

Consequently, one could have Zodiac Goods Ltd. as a company but would have to *trade* under another name. Having said that, in some jurisdictions, even the mere incorporation under a company name (such as the example used here) can amount to actionable trade mark infringement.

Domain Name

Something similar applies to domain name registration. If you secure a .com, .co.uk or .ie domain name registration it does not give you, what's known in legal parlance as "proprietary rights."

You don't have ownership of that for use as a trade mark. So, while you may have "thesilverspoon.com" this it does not confer total exclusivity. It does not stop someone else from using the exact same name *in trade*. There could be lots of *Silver Spoon* restaurants albeit only one .com or of that name.

Its limitations

Rivals could have .ie .biz .org or any of the other domain name designations attaching to their *Silver Spoon* outlets. If you spend money, time and effort building up an enviable business the last thing you want is for someone else to be able to prosper on your coat tails. **Domain name registration does not fully satisfy your wish to have exclusive use of your identity as a trade mark!**

Non exclusive

If you secure a .com or .ie domain name registration, it does not of itself give you the right to object to the use **of** that name by others. For example, mere registration of trident.ie would not give the domain name owner the right to object to the use by another person of TRIDENT as a trade mark.

Business Name Register

It is worth now returning to the issue of Business Name Registration. If you are going to trade under something other than your own name, there is a requirement in law, to register a business name.

Non exclusive

Once again, in so doing, this does not automatically give you permission to use the name as a trade mark nor is it protected. There can be many listings of the same name you choose to use.

Beneficial owner

The main aim of this register is to provide the public with a means to identify the actual owner of the enterprise. For example, if I got ill after having a meal in a restaurant called *The Silver Spoon* and wanted to take legal action against the proprietor I would need to find out his/her name and address.

Register's listings

I would go to the Business Name Register and perhaps find a number of such named restaurants. By scanning the list I would find the location where I had been along with the necessary details as to the owner and a contact address. From this you can see that there can be many exact or similar names on this register. Therefore exclusivity of the name of the restaurant is not gained through this register.

Details of ownership

To recap, this register does not mean you can use the name nor does it protect it. It is there to facilitate the public to find out details of ownership of the business.

Protect your domain name

Those who trade on the Internet and who value domain names should take immediate steps to apply to register them as trade marks. If they fail to do this they may quickly build up recognition in the minds of consumers which other, more alert, marketers may exploit.

(Registering a domain name does not give proprietary rights!)

A rival can "steal" your brand identity

Consider this scenario; you have a new branding (be that trade mark or domain name) which goes, unprotected, into the marketplace. Someone else sees it, thinks "that's clever". They search the trade mark register(s), find the way clear, and then file on their own behalf for a similar class of goods or services. Once the registration comes through (which may take up to 8 months) they can contact you, the original, unregistered user and might be entitled to legally insist that you cease usage of the now *registered* mark, in trade or as a domain name.

You now know the differences between company registration, business name registration and domain name registration.

You know that these do not give you permission to use them in a trade mark fashion nor are they automatically protected.

You will understand that, to gain exclusive use of your brand name, you should go through the trade mark registration process.

In order to begin the process here is a check list to refer to, and follow, as you seek to register your proposed mark.

The following are the <u>critical points</u> in relation to TRADE MARKS registration.

1. Prior to use, it is essential to search the trade marks register in each target market. This will discover any existing names/marks that are the same, *or confusingly similar*, to that which is proposed and where the owner would have a sustainable objection to the new entrant.

2. If the search is clear, then an application should be made to register the mark in all markets where it is intended to use it.

3. Register in all classes of goods and services where it is currently used as well as in classes where there is intent to use. All goods and services are divided into 45 classes. It is advisable to gain exclusivity for the name in whichever classes one is intending to trade in the future. This will obviate the possibility of being frustrated at a later date.

4. The initial life of a registration is 10 years which can be renewed indefinitely each 10 years thereafter.

5. One can apply to register either nationally and/or seek a Community Trade Mark (CTM) registration.

6. The cost of an application, for each class, in Ireland, can be seen on www.patentsoffice.ie. At registration, approximately 6 months later, a further cost arises as detailed on the website.

7. A CTM registration provides exclusive rights to the mark in all member states of the European Union. With just one application, protection can be obtained in all countries of the EU. The cost of an application, which currently covers 3 classes of goods, can be seen on www.oami.europa.eu. Additional classes are extra.

8. When you have secured your CTM registration it is still incumbent on you, when entering a new market, to ensure that your mark does not infringe the existing rights of another trader in that market.

We will refer to this very important checklist from time to time throughout the book.

How are you progressing in coming up with suggestions for trade marks as requested earlier ?

Have you at least possible solutions to some of the tasks listed?

Have you searched the trade mark Registers indicated on page 62 (and on page 6)?

Are your marks pre-empted by others in the same class of goods and services?

This is an excellent exercise to familiarise yourself with the process in creativity and checking.

CHAPTER 3 – CAN YOU USE AND PROTECT YOUR PROPOSED BRANDING?

On the following pages we go through all of the steps that are required to secure the exclusivity you want.

Trade mark use

A trade mark provides exclusive statutory rights so that a rival cannot legally use an identical or *confusingly similar* trade mark to an earlier registration. On the other hand, if you infringe, then all the investment in design, printing and promotion may be wasted.

Golden Rule

Therefore, the golden rule is, do not attempt to market goods or services until the identity

under which you intend to trade has been cleared for use. That is, that it does not conflict with an earlier trade mark registration in the target market.

Search of Trade Mark Registers

It is essential that, before using a new identity, a search is made of the target markets (be that Ireland, the UK, the EU or further afield) to ensure that it does not infringe the rights of others. Expert advice, such as that of a Trade Mark Attorney, is advisable because what appears to be clear to the untrained eye may, in fact, conceal a sustainable objection from a rival.

The registration process

Trade marks are generally registered on a country-by-country basis. However, the Community Trade Mark enables the user by means of a single filing to register its trade mark across the entire territory of the EU.

Four stages

While the application process varies from country to country, most countries provide for four basic stages in its trade mark registration process. These are: Filing by the applicant or his agent, examination by the Patents Office, publication in the Trade Marks Journal (when third parties can submit objections to the registration of the mark) and registration (by the Patent Office).

Filing

Firstly, the user must fill out a trade mark application form. Most countries now provide for online filing, including online payment of application fees. The application will need to include the basic relevant information such as the identification of the trade mark (e.g. word mark, a specimen of any logo etc.), the name and details of the applicant (including if the applicant is a person or company entity), a list of the goods or services for which protection is sought, and payment of the relevant application fees.

Nomination of classes

Trade marks are protected by reference to the classes of goods and/or services in which they will be traded. And so the actual list of these classes must be included by the applicant. Most registries provide information online that identify these classes.

45 separate classes

The system is governed by the Nice Classification which divides goods and services into 45 separate classes comprising thirty-four classes of goods and eleven classes of services. The applicant must nominate his chosen classes (e.g. class 25 covers footwear and clothing while electronic goods such as computers are in class 9.)

Be specific as to intended use

Following a recent EU court decision, registries will no longer automatically allow a user to simply select the standard terms set out in the Nice Classification system. That is the lengthy list of goods and services listed under each class number. As a result, a user may need to liaise with the registry (or consult a professional) in order to put together an acceptable list of goods or services. The general approach is to include those goods/services for which the trade mark is being used or which it is intended to use the mark.

Examination

After a trade mark application has been filed it will be examined by an examiner at the relevant trade mark registry. The extent of examination varies widely from country to country. All registries will check to ensure that basic requirements are met e.g. that the mark is not generic, or offends against public morals, or that the list of goods and services is clear and meets its requirements.

In Ireland

Some registries will also conduct a search for earlier conflicting marks. In some cases, such as Ireland, if a search reveals an earlier conflicting mark, the examiner will object to registration. In such instances, the examiner will write to the applicant to explain the reasons for the objection, giving the applicant an opportunity to respond.

UK, EU and elsewhere

In other countries, such as the UK, the Patent Office will not object to registration if its search uncovers an earlier conflicting mark. It will provide the results of its search to the user and the Examiner will also notify the owners of the earlier marks who may then choose to object to the application.

Publication – opportunity for objection

After an application has been examined and any issues or problems have been dealt with, most countries' registries will publish the application in an official bulletin (or online) for a period of time (usually 3 months) in order to give others an opportunity to object to registration. A registration gives significant exclusive rights to the owner and so it is considered important to ensure that a procedure exists to allow others to object to registration before it matures to registration.

Opposition procedure

In Ireland and before the EU Trade Marks Office, the period - the opposition period - is 3 months. Usually an opposition is lodged by a person who believes that the published mark is too similar to their earlier mark. Some registries, including Ireland, allow for an opposition to be lodged based on a wide variety of grounds. An opposition triggers an opposition procedure which is handled and decided by the registry in which both sides file arguments and which can include an oral hearing. An opposition can delay registration by a few years and, if successful, would mean the refusal of the application by the registry.

Serious matter

This is why a threat of opposition received from a person who has noticed your application upon publication should normally be taken seriously because an opposition, if filed, could seriously threaten the chances of getting a registration and, at the very least, lead to significant delay and costs for the registration process.

Registration

Assuming the mark has been accepted by the registry - following examination - and has not been opposed before the end of the publication period, it will then mature to registration. Most countries do not provide for payment of registration fees and, in such instances, the mark will automatically mature to registration within a short period after the end of the opposition period. The registry will enter the mark on the register and will send the official registration certificate to the owner setting out the details of the registration.

Other countries, such as Ireland, will not register the mark until payment of registration fees. Once registered, the mark will be protected for a fixed period of time which in most countries is ten years from the date of filing.

10 year duration, renewable

The mark can be renewed before the end of each subsequent registration period (i.e. usually every ten years).

Possible cancellation due to non-use

Most countries provide for cancellation of a registered mark which has not been put to use within a few years of registration (usually 5 years from the date of registration) and so it is important to ensure that your registered mark is put to use before the end of this so-called grace period. In addition, in some countries (e.g. the United States), a registration will be struck off unless evidence of use of the mark in trade is filed with the registry.

Be aware of local requirements

It is vital therefore to ensure that you are aware of, and comply with, the use requirements in the countries in which the mark has been registered. Otherwise, the registration might lapse for failure to comply with registry requirements regarding maintenance of a registered trade mark.

Secure your position

Once it has been established that the way is clear the mark should be applied for registration immediately and so secure the position.

Territorial

Remember too that registration is territorial, that is, the protection exists only in the countries in which you have a registration. A registration in the United Kingdom extends to Northern Ireland but the Republic of Ireland is another jurisdiction and therefore requires a separate registration.

Export markets

As has been pointed out already, trade mark protection is territorial so, while you may have your mark legally registered in one country it does not mean you can export goods or services carrying this mark to another country.

Prior rights

Many marketers come unstuck on this point. There have been cases where goods were exported to another country, went on sale, only to find that the exporter or the local agent received a "cease and desist" letter from an indigenous company or its legal advisors. The local company had established prior rights to the trade mark in question.

Foreign language

An offence can be that the trade mark is identical to, or looks, sounds or could be confused with, a trade mark on that local register. On foreign markets, where there are language differences, the conflicting marks may be spelt differently and appear to the eye to be miles apart, but to the ear, be confusingly similar. The overall impression given by the marks at issue is similar!

Local expertise needed

The lesson to be learned therefore is to have the search made by someone who is versed in the language of the target market and thus obviate this regularly occurring problem.

Use of TM and ®

When you begin to use your brand name you may use the TM sign beside it. This simply stands for trade mark albeit that it is unregistered. However, many people believe it does signify registration and may avoid copying it.

In some countries such as Ireland and the UK it is not until you have obtained registration of your trade mark that you can legally use the ® symbol for the registered goods or services (unless, for example, you can show that such use refers to a foreign registration.)

Generally it should only be used in markets where you have been granted registration. The ruling is different in some other countries and local guidance should be sought.

You now know the process to follow to register a trade mark in individual countries.

You know that trade marks are territorial.

However, in the European Union there is one facility that allows you, with just one application, to apply to register your mark across the EU. This refers to the Community Trade Mark (CTM).

CHAPTER 4 – PROTECT YOUR MARK IN THE EU

On the following pages are details that refer to this attractive facility.

Community Trade Mark

In the past when registration was being sought in Europe it was necessary to file country by country. Following the creation of what is now known as the European Union moves were made to provide a short cut. In 1994 a new law was passed that gave us a process whereby a trade mark could be registered Europe wide.

28 Countries

Utilising the Community Trade Mark (CTM) it is now possible, with only one application, to apply to register a trade mark in all 28 countries of the European Union.

Anyone who currently trades, or intends to trade, in the EU in the foreseeable future should seriously consider this option. This facility has an added benefit in that when one successfully secures a CTM registration, it is generally considered that it is only necessary to use the mark in ONE of the 28 countries to initially maintain exclusive protection in all member states. (This is available for five years before being open to challenge on grounds of non-use.)

Huge market

This opens up huge possibilities for the entrepreneur. This marketplace has about 500 million consumers, making it larger than the United States. As new states join the Community the figure will grow even larger.

There are many benefits to be derived from securing a Community Trade Mark.

Here we itemise and examine them. They will illustrate how you can capitalise on this facility if you have the intention to export your product or service.

Not only do you secure your present position but you also ensure that you will be able to expand into other EU markets in future years.

In addition, by having CTM scope you will add to the intrinsic value of your business. A brand that has exclusive rights in the 28 member states (and growing) will be more valuable than one that is exclusive to just one country.

Automatic extension

Any existing CTM will be automatically extended into any new EU entrant state, at no extra cost. That is, provided there is not already a conflicting mark on that member's national register.

National and CTM

The costs involved in both the national and CTM options are very modest. In both cases the period of cover is for an initial 10 years and is renewable.

Three for one

An added bonus with the CTM is that you can have three classes of goods or services registered for the same price as one class. (The EU is currently however considering introducing a separate fee for each class of goods or services.)

Strategic move

Even if expansion into EU countries is not contemplated in the immediate future, one should seek registration in any field of activity where there is a possibility of use.

Additional classes

By covering these additional product/service classes in target markets, the business person gives himself the opportunity to get on with current matters while preserving future options. Moreover, by virtue of multi class filings, in a market place as big as the EU, the intrinsic value of the original trade mark is enhanced.

It is vitally important that you protect your trade mark in your most important market. This is, in the majority of cases, your home country.

Even if you have no intention of exporting, either now or at some future date, do not postpone securing registration on the home front.

Protect home market

Many foreign companies avail of the CTM facility and so it is imperative that indigenous companies protect their trade mark interests by registering at least in their home market.

Burden of proof

Otherwise a rival with *the same or a confusingly similar identity* (where the overall impression given by the marks at issue is similar!) may obtain registration before the indigenous user. Then the burden of proof falls on the local company to prove, in a court of law, that its goodwill is being damaged by the new entrant.

Unregistered rights

This is an expensive and time consuming exercise, (that relies on Common Law/unregistered rights) with no guarantee as to the outcome. The simple way to avoid possible lengthy litigation is to seek to register your trade mark promptly.

Huge opportunities

By the same token if one moves speedily, and secures CTM registration, a plethora of possibilities await. Not only is one faced with a protected environment for personal expansion but also the prospects for franchise arrangements and licensing agreements are enhanced.

Increased value

A large proportion of the value of a company is based on its growth potential, which in turn is enhanced by its brands. It is also very true that brand valuation is therefore now beginning to confirm that brands are centrally important and enormously valuable corporate assets.

Goodwill and loyalty

Brands create trust, goodwill and ultimately loyalty. It is the loyalty that delivers sustainable income to the company that owns the brands.

We have now covered the various considerations and steps associated with the subject matter of trade mark registration.

On the following two pages is a list of reminders to consider when you have chosen a mark to register.

Refer to them EACH time you are about to begin the process of trying to secure registration.

Remember what was said at the beginning of the book...

The following are the <u>critical points</u> in relation to TRADE MARKS.

1. Prior to use, it is essential to search the trade marks register in each target market. This will discover any existing names/marks that are the same, *or confusingly similar*, to that which is proposed and where the owner would have a sustainable objection to the new entrant.

2. If the search is clear, then an application should be made to register the mark in all markets where it is intended to use it.

3. Register in all classes of goods where it is currently used as well as in classes where there is intent to use. All goods and services are divided into 45 classes. It is advisable to gain exclusivity for the name in whichever classes one is intending to trade in the future. This will obviate the possibility of being frustrated at a later date.

4. The initial life of a registration is 10 years which can be renewed indefinitely each decade thereafter.

5. One can apply to register either nationally and/or seek a Community Trade Mark (CTM) registration. The cost

of an application, for each class, in Ireland, can be seen on www.patentsoffice.ie. At registration, approximately 6 months later, a further cost arises.

6. A CTM registration provides exclusive rights to the mark in all member states of the European Union. With just one application, protection can be obtained in all countries of the EU. The cost of an application, which currently covers 3 classes of goods, can be seen on www.oami.europa.eu. Additional classes are extra.

7. When you have secured your CTM registration it is still incumbent on you, when entering a new market, to ensure that your mark does not infringe the existing rights of another trader in that market.

CHAPTER 5 – THE CREATIVE PROCESS

We now return to the creative process of devising a trade mark for the goods or service you wish to brand and protect.

In so doing you are now more fully armed with all that you have learned from the previous pages.

You know that to obtain registration of your new branding you have to comply with the stipulations itemised on those earlier pages.

With these in mind <u>you</u> start to work on the daunting task of being truly creative.

The empty page

The challenge is to create a name for a new offering and you are faced with a blank sheet of paper.

You have to devise an identity that will sit happily on the product or service and will be attractive and memorable to the consumer.

The name need not have any relationship to the product or service to be branded.

Un-associated

It is possible to choose a name that has no apparent association with the product or service and start with that. For instance, if the product was a new type of vacuum cleaner, why not call it a PINEAPPLE?

You may think this is a ludicrous suggestion but if I asked you if you had an APPLE at home, would you think of a computer?

Recognition

Now APPLE is probably one of the best recognised trade marks in the world and the company is the wealthiest as I write this piece. It enjoys not only use of the name for the product but also the company and the website.

So don't dismiss such a suggestion of an un-associated name out of hand. But it took many years and lots of dollars spent in promoting the company and its products to reach the recognition level it enjoys today.

My preference is for a name that alludes to the product or service. This captures the attention and interest of the consumer. It also makes it more memorable.

Covert reference

I much prefer having a covert, or hidden, reference to the product or service I am branding. This has many benefits. It makes it easier to register as a trade mark because the Official Examiner in the Patents Office (the government office where trade marks are submitted for registration) will not allow obviously descriptive marks. It is just one of the many stipulations that have to be contended with when lodging a mark for registration.

Do not think of using something that directly describes that which you are marketing.

Avoid the obvious

The obvious

Therefore SLICED CHEESE will not be accepted as a trade mark for, sliced cheese. On the other hand EASI SINGLES meets the covert association angle and identifies cheese that is ready sliced.

Use of a clever trade mark can lead to lots of free publicity because it catches the eye of journalists and media people.

Free publicity and PR

The other benefits to which I refer to above relate to the free promotional and PR potential that can be had from having a cleverly devised trade mark. This is particularly advantageous if there is not a huge amount of finance available at the outset for promoting the new brand with advertising support.

CHAPTER 6 – CLEVER MARKS ATTRACT ATTENTION

On the following pages are examples of how, by creating a clever trade mark, the attention of the consumer was immediately captured. It was also the ideal platform for widespread media coverage.

These will act as a guide, and perhaps an inspiration, for you when you undertake the task of trade mark creation.

Be clever

This is easier said than done. So let me digress slightly to give an example from my past which is set out in a series of articles I wrote at the time.

Many forms of trade mark

In so doing let me begin by explaining that there are many kinds of trade mark not readily known to the public at large. Yet they are influenced by them day after day without them realising it. These include shapes, sounds, colours and even smells. I include some of these in the article that follows.

The various forms a trade mark can take include;

word(s)

logotype

symbol

slogan

sound

shape

colour

smell

These can be registered internationally.

Later, I will go into each one in greater detail so that you will be able to fully understand, and exploit them, to your advantage.

Likewise with the essential steps that need to be taken to clear the chosen mark for use, and then to register them in the target markets.

CHAPTER 7 – EXAMPLES OF CLEVER USE

Beginning below on this page is an article that was part of a series. It refers to a seminar I delivered to a large audience of business people.

I have added bold statements throughout the article to emphasise each of the various forms trade mark registration can take.

It will also assist you when revisiting the subject and working on your own project.

"STOP TALKING AND DO SOMETHING"
For some time now a lot of you have been reading these articles and learning from the subject matter covered. It is heartening to receive very positive and encouraging comments from diverse sources. People write that they

look forward to reading the articles and are able to relate to items that appeared in earlier issues.

In certain instances, some of the advice and guidance was used to telling effect. This prompts me to pick up on this point and tell about something I did, where I put my money where my mouth is, so to speak!

How is it done?
It is likely that some readers learn to understand the possibilities relating to trade marks, and the like. They find it less easy to see how they might exploit the free publicity and P R potential that I refer to time and time again.

Here's how
So I thought I would give some concrete examples of how this could be brought into play and how a business could be created. Moreover, to back up my oft repeated claim that publicity can be had from clever use of branding, I decided to do just that!

A case in point

Some years ago I was asked to participate in a seminar in Northern Ireland and make a presentation on intellectual property rights. The audience would be comprised of a cross section of businesses, support agencies and advertising/creative personnel.

Grab their attention

To have general appeal I needed something that all could relate to, so I chose some products that all of them might purchase and use in everyday life.

Imaginary products

These products did not already exist nor was I actually in the business of producing them. All I wanted to do was demonstrate how they could come into existence and be the basis for an on-going enterprise.

But memorable

They would catch the imagination of the target market, be immediately memorable, protectable and attract a great deal of media attention. All on a meagre budget!

Laced through the presentation would be all the steps one should take in such an exercise and the part intellectual property should play in the evolution.

Buy into

And so a large eclectic audience gathered in Belfast early one morning to watch me fall flat on my face or be impressed with a proposition they could buy into, if it was reality.

New aftershave and perfume

I told them I was about to launch two new products into their market. A man's aftershave and a perfume for ladies. I did not have any promotional budget so I needed to get as much attention, free publicity and P R as I could muster. I wanted to get the media interested in the products and achieve extensive press coverage, radio and TV interviews. My intention was to use intellectual property, from a sales and marketing perspective, to do just that.

Here's how to use intellectual property rights to grab attention, promote the products, protect the branding and position it to get free media coverage.

Unusual shape

One of the first slides projected onto the screen beside me showed an unusual, nicely styled bottle. I explained that it would be filled with the new aftershave that had been specially created for this market.

Registered as a trade mark

This shape of the bottle I was going to use was protected by trade mark registration. (The unusual shape of the Coca-Cola bottle enjoys trade mark registration too.) Therefore no rival of mine could legally have an identical or confusingly similar shape to mine.

You can register shapes as trade marks

Symbol

Then a stylised castle was flashed up on the screen. This would appear on the bottle by way of a symbol for the range as it evolved. This too would be a protected mark and form part of the intellectual property portfolio that was emerging.

You can register a symbol as a trade mark

Colours

The box, into which the bottle would be packaged, had an unusual and very attractive series of colour combinations. This arrangement of colours was capable of registration.

You can register a colour(s) as a trade mark

The name/trade mark

Then we came to the name. A lot of research had gone into the creation of a brand that would have instant recognition and a good resonance in the marketplace.

In addition, it would have to be easy to pronounce, be memorable and be definitely something around which advertising, PR and free publicity could be built.

A number of names had been considered before one stood out from the rest as a clear winner.

Undertake a trade mark search in your target markets.

Trade mark clearance

The first thing to do then was to have a search made of the appropriate trade mark registers to ensure it did not infringe the existing rights of others. Once the all-clear was to hand (and that only took a week) an application to register was made.

Choose a trade mark that will engage the consumer

Registered trade mark

The screen was then filled with the chosen brand – **STORMINT**. That raised a chuckle from the audience. They immediately recognised that it was a play on the name of their House of Parliament in Northern Ireland. Every newspaper, radio and TV report carries daily reference to **STORMONT** the seat of government there.

You can register a word(s) as a trade mark

Stylised word

The word STORMINT was treated in a stylised manner. This is known as a logotype. In trade mark jargon it is referred to as a figurative mark.

You can register a logotype as a trade mark. It is referred to as a figurative mark.

Slogan

We then covered the idea of having a slogan for the product. It is now possible to register slogans as trade marks and these have the same breath of cover that the other forms of trade marks enjoy.

The strapline used was " STORMINT aftershave, **a whiff of political intrigue"** and yes, we had already applied to register that slogan.

You can register a slogan as a trade mark

McDonald's "I'm lovin' it".

NIKE "Just do it".

PEPSI "Take it to the Max".

Sound mark

I told the audience that you can also obtain exclusive rights to sounds. For instance, the sound of a Harley Davidson motor cycle was a trade mark and no rival cycle could have a similar sound for the protected goods.

Audience participation

Now, I said, I cannot afford to get 200 people into a recording studio to record a sound mark but as all you are here, would you please help me out?

I told them that Dave here, on sound, had agreed to help me. On the count of three, would the audience please slap the sides of the face 3 times, stretch out their hands and shout STORMINT?

And do you know, they all did it! We then had a recording of their hands clapping their faces and the cry of the brand name.

You can register a sound as a trade mark

DIRECTLINE Insurance – The sound of a bugle. INTEL The sound of a chime.

After the men, the ladies!

This is just one of the products shown that day.
I followed the same format for the perfume product.

The name I used for it was DERRIER. This was a pun
on the well-known song "The Londonderry Air."
In this case I had the audience sing the first few bars
of the song, which they willingly did, and we recorded it.

**Already, you see the publicity potential that this
clever branding holds.**

Audience reaction
After the entire presentation the Chairman of a UK
public company who was in the audience approached
me. He said that was not intellectual property per se, it
was pure sales and marketing.

He told me that from now on, every time he passed by
Stormont he would remember STORMINT. And if there
was anyone in the car with him he would slap his face
and relate the story of the hypothetical product.

They wanted to buy the hypothetical products.

In addition, I had many of the audience approach me at the conclusion of the seminar and ask to purchase some of the products.

You can do the same as me!

Let's move on
Now that you have got the general picture and an overview of what can be done we can get down to working through the process of branding a product.

Here's how you can begin the task of creating a trade mark. One that incorporates the benefits that attach to clever branding.

As I said earlier, I prefer the covert, or hidden, approach to selecting a trade mark. The article you have just read highlights some of the advantages to be had from this strategy and can do much for the promotion of your project.

Aim to create a mark that will resonate with the targeted consumer.

A memorable inference

To this end, you need to do some lateral thinking. You cannot hope to get exclusive rights, through registration, to a purely descriptive title. You must find a way that infers an association with what it is you want to brand. You also want something that will resonate with your targeted consumer. Something that is easy for them to remember.

Start to list

The best place to start is by listing all of the words that could be associated with the product or service in question. At the outset, you will come up with words that fill the bill but are problematic because they fall into the descriptive category.

Different approach

But, with perseverance, you will discover alternatives that are more likely to have a chance of success. During this process you will refine your thinking and begin to look at possibilities from a different angle. When this happens you can be confident that you are beginning to develop the necessary skills to create effective trade marks.

Avoid the obvious and explore words that do not have a direct reference but hold some association

This does not come easily. It is a hard graft but is well worth the effort. There is huge satisfaction in knowing you have "cracked it" when the word emerges that is just right for the job.

Here's a challenge to get you started

This is an actual case study where I had come up with a suitable branding for new sort of dog's kennel. Because of the novelty of design it could be protected by way of design registration.

What name would you create to brand a new design of dog's kennel?

Distinctive difference

As dog's kennels are well known and established as such, I did not want this new, radically improved version labelled with the same title as the old ones.

If such were the case potential customers could phone around asking for the price of _a kennel_ and be offered the standard alternatives at lower prices than those at which mine would be pitched. As mine was distinctively better, incorporating a litany of extra benefits, it needed a distinctively different brand name.

Review the list

So let's begin to create the list of everything you can think of that might fit. Start writing! When you have exhausted the list, review it and strike off all those that are either descriptive, or bordering on being descriptive.

Eliminate any names that you listed that are descriptive or have a direct reference to the product.

Do the same to those that are not attractive to the eye or the ear. Ditto to those that have no commercial ring to them. With those that have survived so far be very honest with yourself when asking "do they have a true link with the product we are going to promote?"

Reject those names that are not attractive to the eye and/or the ear.

Look for the logic

If you have a number of probables then you are really making progress. Look back at the long list you began with and appreciate how many of them were really non-starters. See how your mind, and logic, developed as you went through the exercise.

You now have ones that you believe fit the bill. Rank them in order of preference.

Name creation technique

Before turning the page and discovering the name I settled on please spend a long time examining your own efforts. This is only the beginning of the journey we are going to take together as we explore, by way of a myriad of examples, how name creation can be something you can master.

Examples, the best tutor

I have found, with all of the people I have helped over the years, that they grasp best, and comprehend more quickly what's needed, when they are exposed to a litany of names that have been created.

When you see the names that have been created for a wide range of products and services it will become clearer to you how the covert reference comes into play.

Thinking pattern

For that reason, we will go through very many stories of challenges that were faced, for a wide variety of products, and the trade marks that were generated for them. In each case you will see for yourself, not only the result but also appreciate the thinking behind their creation and selection. In this way you will begin to develop the required thinking pattern.

Refine your approach

From then on you will refine your approach and start to improve on your skill. Over time you will develop your own particular methodology.

Your own system

There is no one secret formula. What works best for you is what you're after. Achieve it and you've got it made!

Remember the challenge?

> *Task 3: You are tasked with the job of coming up* *with a suitable trade mark for a new design of kennel* *for dogs.*

Here is the name chosen for the branding of the dog's kennel. See how it has that covert reference.

The answer

The name I created for this was **BARKHOUSE.** Now let's examine the logic behind its selection. The kennel is made of timber (although it need not be limited to that material); mention the word BARK and first two things that will pop into a person's mind are *timber and dog*.

Covert reference

Stop someone in the street, or even in a DIY store, and say BARKHOUSE and they won't immediately think you are referring to a kennel. Even if the test is done with the product in close proximity it will not be taken as an obvious direct reference to the goods. Therefore the branding has the desired covert reference to the product. Not a purely descriptive title. It is a suitable word for trade mark registration so that you can enjoy exclusive use of the title.

When you have a suitable name, the search and registration process can begin.

Search and registration

Once you have settled on a mark that fits the bill you have to continue with the search and registration process.

Here is another example of a range of trade marks created for a range of new products

New product range

On another occasion, towards the end of a seminar I was delivering, I said to the audience that we would now create a branding for a range of new products. We would use all that had been learned during the seminar.

A WOW brand

The aim would be to come up with a branding that would be a wow, project the products onto the minds of the consumer and enjoy a higher price point than usual. It should also attract free publicity.

We picked a product sector that had been around for years and presented a real challenge.

I asked for suggestions of mundane products, ones that were already in existence and were somewhat lack lustre.

Among the shouts came, *sandwiches*, they have been done to death and are on sale everywhere!

Range of sandwiches

OK, let's create a range of sandwiches that will stand out from the rest, get the public talking about them, and, more importantly, buying them. They would be retailed at a higher price than what was presently available. We will use protectable branding to do just that and, at the same time, be a vehicle for free publicity and PR.

We would create a brand that made the products stand out from the rest and capture consumer and media attention.

Disbelief

The look on the face of the audience was one of disbelief. Here was a guy who was really biting off more than he could chew. His challenge was to come up with a branding that would project his offering above all that was there already, and he wanted to get a higher price for them! No way!

Let the challenge begin

My first thought was to come up with a proposition that would lend itself to strong branding. One that would have line extensions that could be registered as trade marks in its many different forms.

We would use the many forms of trade mark registration to achieve our aims.

Exotic/erotic

I told the audience that we would produce a range of sandwiches that would have the very unusual tagline

"Exotic sandwiches with erotic fillings."

So I wrote that on my flip chart. That would be the subtitle and slogan for the new range.

Remember, you can register a slogan as a trade mark

Now, let's choose a trade mark. After an interesting and exciting debate the name I settled on was PASSION.

PASSION

"Exotic sandwiches with erotic fillings."

You can register a word as a trade mark

Someone shouted "what about Ration of Passion?" Great, we can use that as part of our promotional activity.

Big red lips

The sandwiches will be sold in plastic boxes. On the end side of the box we will print big "Marilyn Monroe" red lips. So, when displayed on shelves, you will see a long line of red lips that really stand out. On these we will add the name of each sandwich variety.

You can register that design as a trade mark

Individual names

So that the customers could order their particular favourites we decided to give each of them a name. Each one had to be capable of being registered as a trade mark. Here are just four.

LETTUCEDOIT
BIG HUG
FRENCE KISS
and **LOVE BITE.**

Each of these can be registered as a trade mark

None of them have a direct reference to the sandwiches nor can they be considered to be descriptive.

Radio

When we had some funds, we would have a radio commercial. It would start with the sound of a long kiss. You can register sounds as trade marks. The commercial would start with the sound of a long kiss. Then, after the sound of a kiss, the voiceover would say "Did you get your ration of PASSION today? Exotic sandwiches with erotic fillings. Rush out to a shop near you. You'll love getting a BIG HUG and a FRENCH KISS."

You can register a sound as a trade mark

Audience reaction

By now the place was jumping. They really bought into the concept. Everyone could see the huge potential that the branding alone was giving to the new venture.

Every element of the branding caught the imagination of the audience. They wanted to buy the products right away.

Comments

Some of the comments were as follows: "You can imagine a chap shouting out of his car window to his mate, "Hey, did you get your ration of passion?" Or someone in an office saying "Go down to Dave he has a bloody big love bite." Or going into a shop and asking the assistant for a French kiss.

One member of the audience said "If you had any of them for sale this evening I'd buy a few to see if they worked for my Missus."

Variety of trade marks

The lesson to be learned is that most of the elements we created during that session would be capable of being registered as trade marks. These would include word marks, sound marks and design registrations.

Extension of the branded products can involve input from customers and they can be rewarded

Consumer involvement

In addition, by the use of this clever creativity, the new range would attract lots of free publicity. Further customer attraction and involvement would be generated by way of consumer competition. They could be asked to suggest names for new sandwiches to be added to the range. Winning names, capable of being registered, would receive a prize.

Novelty can justify a higher retail price and open up franchise possibilities

Exclusivity

The novelty of the branding would allow for a higher price point. There is also franchise potential for the overall concept. This consideration is given added strength by the capability of registering so many elements of the branding thereby ensuring exclusivity of use.

You will see from the development of this product range how the names add interest to the individual

sandwiches and fit neatly into the overall brand name.

Thought process

This story exemplifies and reinforces the thought process that you must employ when you are creating a brand. You must chose words that do not have a direct reference to the goods themselves.

Added value

The bonus is that they add interest and value to your product. They make the product name memorable and have the advantage of lending themselves to free publicity because of the fun element. It is the type of thing that could become viral because it catches the imagination of the target market.

The same logic was used in the development of branding for an entirely different product sector.

Task4: Fashion jewellery whose trade mark will exude expense and exclusivity.

Jewellery

A different project was for a company planning to produce a range of fashion jewellery to rival the then market leader in the United Kingdom. These products were referred to as fashion jewellery because they were not aimed at the expensive, high end market sector.

You can infer superior status if you use the right choice of expression.

Designer

The first, clever part of the strategy was to call our range

"Designer jewellery"

This gave it a perceived step above the regular, established, *fashion* jewellery. Even though ALL jewellery is designed, if you're first to grab the title "designer" you gain a foothold in the mind of the consumer. You elevate your product to a higher plateau.

Cachet

The name we chose for the new range was CACHET. This is a French word, although commonly used in English. It that has one dictionary definition that reads "An indication of approval carrying great prestige." We produced the word in an attractive logotype style and, as such, was capable of registration as a trade mark.

The logic of using a French word and emphasising the allure that goes with it elevated the range and its perceived value.

Subtitle

We heightened the status of the brand by using a number of other clever means. We quoted yet another piece from a dictionary;

Cachet, n.F.stamp (fig) distinguishing mark, evidence of authenticity.

We added an advertising line that proclaimed,

"Only the best deserves the imprimatur CACHET."

Then lastly, to reflect the beauty of the product, albeit at an affordable price, we had a tagline, **"Designs that are breath-taking, prices that are not."**

To further illustrate how clever branding can benefit products and services in all sectors of the marketplace the following list is compiled.

Wide range

And now for a wide range of diverse brand names that illustrate how each one is suitable for the product in question. In some instances the word itself is registerable as a trade mark, in others, it may be that a logotype was used to gain registration and exclusivity of use.

Averlopes

A name created for the giant Avery Company for use on its special security envelopes produced by Avery Labels.

This is a novel combination of part of the word Avery being merged with the word envelope to produce the fanciful trade mark AVERLOPES.

BUNDYS

This is a totally meaningless word but with the happy connotations using the product itself as a prefix. It was for a new range of bread buns. It also had a tagline that proved very popular with children, for whom it was aimed, "BUNDYS *more fun than a bun.*"

Task 5: For the kiddies market a trade mark for an innovative sweet product.

This identity was for sweet confections that provided the impression of "lift off" and high tech. The product itself had spaceship features that were echoed in the chosen trade mark.

The logotype used here incorporated an illustration of a bird sitting on the last L of the name. It was a name for a wild bird feeder product emphasising its attractant nature by suggestion.

By using extensions to the two Ws in the name, a graphic was produced which mimicked the bounce of microwaves. It was a trade mark for a range of microwave cooking dishes that identified the concept of the micro-wave oven in graphic terms.

This is a combination of "Ri" (Gaelic for King) and Claddagh, an area in Galway, renowned in days gone by for its fisherfolk. We also incorporated the famous Claddagh ring in the design of the logotype.

RECALL

At the time, a new cream was being developed by a client who claimed it would negate the advancing facial lines of age. Supported by the tagline "Youth's eternal secret captured in a cream" RECALL was to be the wonder product that aided you to look young again.

MEGAPOLIS

"The only computer based business game in the world." As it was heralded then, this was one of a range of "solid state, no moving parts" technology to revolutionise the board-game world. Sister products were MARINEATTACK and TANKATTACK.

BULLETS

Tough toffee bullets – just bite and reload.

Task 6: A leading ladies fashion design house requires a distinctive trade mark that highlights the different colours as the seasons change.

WATERCOLOURS

A new fashion experience from a leading ladies fashion design house. The very distinctive logotype was constant but it was portrayed in different colours as the seasons changed. Therefore it was always compatible with the colour-ways of the clothes to which it was attached.

FIELD DAY

This was an identity for a company that grew and marketed fruit and vegetable products. It had a tagline "The pick of the day's crop."

SUPERDAWN

A mark for a rival company in the same sector of activity.

A keep fit studio that offered a wide range of activities from aerobics to martial arts. The exercising figures spell out the first word of the name.

This was a case where the client was insistent on retaining the name even though it had the shortcoming of being a common surname. It was for a bakery that sold product, in the main, through it hot bread shops. The logotype is comprised of the name in a "baked" imagery.

Task 8: A selection of sea food products needs a trade mark that relates to that industry.

This was the branding for a services company that tended to the wide-spread needs of the fishing industry.

By examining all of these examples you will gain an insight into the logic behind their creation. You will see how the branding compliments the product. You will recognise how direct descriptiveness was avoided.

In reviewing them you see how the thought process was challenged so that the chosen trade mark alluded to the product.

The consumer was always to the forefront of the task, it was the search for a branding that grabs the consumer's attention and makes it easy to pronounce and remember.

You can train your mind to work in the same way.

Guideline examples

Throughout this book I have provided examples of marks that have been produced that suit the products or services to which they are attached. But the examples also illustrate the mind-set that we must have when attacking the challenge. If you follow the logic and style indicated then you will build a knowledgebase and the ability to create.

Creating a suitable trade mark is not a simple task. You need practice and perseverance. But success is very satisfying and rewarding.

Not simple

The selection of a brand name for a new product might seem the easiest step in the marketing process. In fact it is one of the most difficult. The chosen name must be appropriate for the product. It must be easily recalled by the intended consumer. It cannot be the same as or resemble a brand or name that is already registered or in use by a competitor.

Choose a mark that meets the requirements for registration of a trade mark. Revisit the section that explains the process.

Easy to register

Most important of all it must be easy to register as a trade mark. Trying to reconcile each of these requirements calls for an understanding and application of skills that relate to marketing, product design and trade mark law.

Do not use a mark until you have searched the appropriate trade mark registers to ensure you are not infringing the rights of third parties.

No searches

Frequently products are launched under a brand name without the basic understanding of what is required. No preliminary searches having first been carried out to ensure that the mark is free for use. Then, if the mark is free for use, that it has been filed for registration in the target markets.

Do not export branded goods until you have established that prior rights do not already exist in that market.

Law suits

Unfortunately, many companies unthinkingly export goods only to find that they infringe a foreign registration. Law suits are then initiated by irate competitors.

CHAPTER 8 – PITFALLS TO AVOID

There is another side to the branding story of which you should be aware. I referred to it in another article I penned some time back.

Genericide or killing a brand with your own hands.

There is a long list of words used in everyday conversation that once were the exclusive property of individual companies. These became part of common parlance for a variety of reasons but mainly through neglect on the part of their owners.

Avoid this mistake

It is vitally important that today's marketeers do not fall into the same trap but are forever vigilant in protecting their intellectual property.

This may sound like a grandiose term yet it embraces such important intangible assets as trade marks, including logotypes symbols and the like.

Valuable property

Just as other forms of property, buildings, paintings or furniture, can appreciate in value and be sold for a higher profit, so also can trade marks increase dramatically in importance and value.

Well known defaulters

Many may be surprised to learn that *Zip, Escalator and Nylon* were trade marks owned by those who invented these products. However, because they did not police their use in commerce, the words were used to describe the article or function rather than identify the particular manufacturer.

Generic

Therefore they became generic and a form of commercial suicide came into being with the cleverly coined term "Genericide".

Endangered marks

How many times have we said "I must hoover this room" or "Give me a loan of your biro"?
When really what we intend to say is "I must vacuum clean this room" and "Give me a loan of your ball point pen". If Messrs' *Hoover* and *Biro* were not on their guard they run the risk of having their brands become generic too.

Official caution

To quote from the European Community Trades Mark CTM) regulations "If, in consequence of acts or inactivity of the proprietor, the trade mark has become the common name in the trade for a product or service in respect of which it is registered.......the rights of the proprietor of the trade mark shall be declared to be revoked on application to the Office".

Alert others

Therefore provident owners of marks ensure that their brands are not used for advertising purposes as verbs or nouns in sentences. They advise their sales staff and agents to be on the lookout for misuse in promotional material created by third parties such as wholesalers and retailers of their products. Even though the incorrect use may be innocent and well intentioned it can still have damaging effect on the brand.

Identify and distinguish

In some instances the name can become so well-known and established in the minds of consumers that it fails to fulfil its primary purpose, that of identifying and distinguishing the goods or services of a particular supplier.

Two more fallers

As a result, we can add to the list above by highlighting *gramophone and linoleum* and ask how else would you describe such items if you did not use these terms?

CHAPTER 9 – FAMOUS BRANDS

Product types too

Two other interesting losses of sovereignty, where loss of designation status, has led to commonality of use are in the cheese category. Cheddar, which used to describe a method of making along with the resultant product, of a cheese from that part of England has now lost its exclusivity.

Headache?

Another name with which all will be familiar is *Aspirin.* Its history is worth recalling for a number of reasons. In the early days when patents were being sought the applicants used original names to identify their inventions.

These subsequently were to become known as non-proprietary names and resulted in complications, as in this case. The lifetime of a patent is 20 years and when that period expires anyone is free to manufacture the product. Moreover, if the invention has not been marketed under a registered trade mark, the name of the previously patented product is also free for use. Such were the circumstances surrounding our well known tablet.

Loss of exclusivity

Aspirin evolves from its full German title *Acetylirte Spirsaure (*acetylated spiraeic acid) to produce *Aspir* with *in* added for good measure. Bayer AG manufactured the product but lost exclusive rights to the name *in some countries* when the patent ran out and the courts ruled that as it had no other name it was in fact generic. Other firms were then free to manufacture the product and market it under that name.

Rival emerges

An Australian chemist, George Nicholas, succeeded in making his own version. As it happened Bayer had never applied for a patent in Australia so there would have been no breach of patent. Nicholas firstly marketed his product under the *Aspirin* trade mark. Initially sales were poor and this was put down to the harmful connotations associated with the name's German association.

Name change

The trade mark was quickly changed to *Aspro* and sales began to take off. In 1927 the Aspro Company was formed which by 1956 became Aspro-Nicholas.

It is also worth noting that in Ireland, the Stirling Winthrop Group Ltd v. Farbenfabriken Bayer AG case, details a long saga of the tussle for the Bayer name, its cross symbolism and *Aspirin's* involvement. The case ran from June 27, 1967 to July 28, 1968.

Be warned

The lesson to be learned from all this is, firstly make sure all of your trade marks are registered. (Remember having a limited liability company name or a business name registration does not give statutory trade mark protection). Then ensure that the marks are never used in a generic fashion. Otherwise the results can be fatal!

CHAPTER 10 – REGISTERING TRADE MARKS AS DOMAIN NAMES

DOMAIN NAMES whatyemaycallem.

In the early days of Internet domain name registration there was much concern being expressed with regards to establishing rights to the lawful use of domain names. Opportunists abounded intent on making a killing while bona fide owners worried about their identities being usurped by others. Governing bodies in the area of Intellectual Property addressed these issues back then and the following will provide some insight into developments at that time.

In 1997, the U S government decided to privatise the handling of domain addresses. A company by the name of Network Solutions Inc. (NSI) was given an exclusive licence to register the top level domain names of .com .org and .net.

As a result of a white paper a number of new entities were created. One of these, the Internet Corporation for Assigned Names and Numbers (ICANN) is a not-for-profit set-up whose sole aim is to encourage and co-ordinate the technical and policy details of Internet management on a community-wide basis. This led to some uneasiness with NSI which has largely been resolved. Moreover, NSI now shares the three types of Top Level Domain names (TLDs) with more than 100 accredited registrars in various countries.

There are three advisory bodies to ICANN, one of which is the Domain Name Supporting Organisation (DNSO) and trade marks and other intellectual property matters fall under its aegis. Trade mark owners have long been concerned about unlawful use of their marks as domain names and cybersquatting plus the length of time it takes to take transgressors to court.

In order to short cut this procedure ICANN appointed the World Intellectual Property Organisation to resolve such disputes and from the beginning of the year 2000 three Uniform Dispute Resolution Policy (UDRP) groups came into being. If the owner of a trade mark finds an identical or confusingly similar domain name to his name, UDRP can be a quick and easy forum for resolving the issue.

However it should be noted that the UDRP is only applicable in certain, defined cases. These are:
1. when the name is identical or confusingly similar to a trade mark;
2. when the applicant has no rights or legitimate interests in the proposed domain name;
3. when the domain name is registered and is being used in bad faith.

Some examples of bad faith include –
1. A domain name is registered to prevent the rightful owner of the trade mark from using it;

2. to disrupt a competitor; for the purpose of selling it on for profit; to create confusion.

The average cost per complaint is $1.000 and a case is likely to take no more than two months to proceed to fruition. While this is not seen as the panacea to all ills, it nevertheless offers an alternative to the courts which will, of course, be required for the more obstinate cases.

The most important point to note is the desirability to hold a trade mark registration. Without such a registration the avenues open to redress any transgressions from third parties are seriously curtailed. In such instances one must rely on the tort of *Passing Off* which can be an expensive and time consuming exercise involving recourse to the courts of law.

Let's for a moment return to the challenge I set for you on page 33.

You were asked to come up with suitable trade marks for 7 different client product lines.

How did you get on?

Compare your creations to those mentioned in the book. Look at the pros and cons, as you see them, of what I have set down. Put yours up alongside them and make critical comparisons.

CHAPTER 11 – INTERESTING STORIES OF HOW NAMES AND BRANDS CAME INTO EXISTENCE

How many of the most recognised trade marks came into being.

ALL TOGETHER NOW, YAHOO

In 1995, two young Americans, who had been developing an idea for a couple of years, finally launched an internet server company that was to become a household name and now receives millions of visitors each month.

Jerry Yang, then 26 years of age, and a fellow Stanford University graduate David Filo, two years his senior, wanted to assist web surfers find their way around the world-wide web. The new phenomenon was growing by the second. It was almost impossible to comprehend and select all that was becoming available on the Net. The boys' business plan was to produce software which would categorise and collate everything. This would enable the surfer to easily find what was needed.

The name they chose for the enterprise was Yahoo and this web portal is now operational in 15 countries and has a market capitalisation of $70 billion. Yang, who has just turned 31 is worth $7.5 billion, (yes, that's *billion*, not *million*) and so is his partner David.

The dictionary definition of Yahoo is "a coarse person of bestial passion and habits" but in the case of the young billionaires it was chosen as an acronym for "Yet another hierarchical officious oracle". Not a lot of people know that!

THE BUSINESS WORLD IS NO GARDEN OF EDEN.

APPLE

Steve Jobs, the inventor of the "Apple" computer decided on this name for a variety of reasons.

He had been working on an apple farm and considered this to be the most perfect fruit. In addition, he was a great fan of the Beatles, whose record company was called Apple Corps and of course he knew all about Sir Isaac Newton's inspiration for his theory on gravity.

Jobs and his fellow inventor, Steve Wozniak, had great difficulty coming up with a suitable name for their end product. Finally they agreed that if they could not come up with a better name for their invention, they would call it Apple. This they did, funnily enough, on April 1, 1976. (Steve had been working in an orchard as a summer job.)

The original concept for the symbol included Newton, the tree and an "Apple Computer" banner. Jobs thought this to be too fussy and a more simple design would provide a stronger branding.

A second attempt depicted a whole apple but this could be confused with an orange so a bite was taken out of it and, viola, we have the now famous mark!

INSPIRATION CAME FROM THE LARGEST AND LONGEST RIVER IN THE WORLD.

Amazon

Amazon.com commenced its virtual business in July 1995 offering the fastest, easiest way to buy books. Since then it has exploded into the largest selection of almost anything from books to videos, games, electronics, gardening needs to art auctions.

In the early years more than 17 million people in 160 countries had bought on-line from Amazon. It has taken equity interests in other Internet retailers such as drugstore.com, for health and beauty products; HomeGrocer.com, for home delivery of groceries and Pets.com, the largest pet supplies company on the Internet.

The man who started it all and still heads up the multi-billion concern is Jeff Bezos. Jeff has been Chairman of the Board of the Company since founding it in 1994 and Chief Executive Officer since May 1996.

From December 1990 to June 1994, he was employed by D.E. Shaw & Co., a Wall Street investment firm, becoming Senior Vice President in 1992. From April 1988 to December 1990, Jeff was employed by Bankers Trust Company, becoming Vice President in February 1990.

Jeff received his B.S. in Electrical Engineering and Computer Science, Summa Cum Laude, from Princeton University.

He named his enterprise Amazon after one of the largest and longest rivers in the world which reflected the same attributes as his on-line offering.

WHO'S FOR COFFEE?

STARBUCKS

The Starbucks Coffee Company was formed by three college students who created the Starbucks name and logo after discovering classic, nautical characters in literature and art. The two-tailed siren depicted in their logo and packaging is a creature of strength and power, and is common in medieval adventure tales.

The company's name is derived from Captain Starbuck, the first mate and adventurer named in Herman Melville's novel, Moby Dick.

A little bit of history.

Back in the 90s

A trade mark name alone can be extremely hard to value but some pointers can be gleaned from the following; when the telecom ORANGE was floated on the stock market the branding alone was estimated to be worth $200 million; when Nestle bought Rowntree the bulk of the $4.5 billion paid was in recognition of the Rowntree brands.

What price Amazon? When the company had an estimated market capitalisation in excess of $20 billion its pro forma loss for 1999 was $390 million!

Enterprises were being purchased for far in excess of their book value because of their attractive IP. It is revealing to study the percentage value of IP (back then) to the total market value of some new and old businesses; for example, Amazon.com 98%; The GAP 90%; McDonalds 73% and Disney 68%.

The Walt Disney Company held no direct ownership in Tokyo Disneyland. However, it licensed the use of its characters for five per cent of the gate money and ten per cent of the sales of merchandise, food and beverages. A Japanese bank associated with underwriting the theme park remarked at the time "Mickey Mouse is a better risk than the US government".

The Coca Cola Corporation once had a market capitalisation that was valued at circa $115 billion when its net book value was nearer to 10% of this figure.

GUN HO

One famous "gun man" trade mark made the headlines for a completely different set of reasons. Uzi Gal, died at the age of 79. It was he who gave his name to name the rapid shooting firearm that had recorded sales in excess of $2bn since its introduction half a century ago.

Unlike the Russian army general, Kalashnikov, whose name was also currently headlines because of alleged copyright infringement associated with the AK47, Mr Gal never wanted his moniker to identify his invention. In fact he tried to stop such branding but his objection was denied by the Israeli Military Industries, the concern that manufactures the gun.

Still more interesting snippets, stories and backgrounds relating to well-known trade marks

These include trade marks that encompass sounds and smells to further identify the particular brands to which they are attached

Cheeky coffee

One of the biggest selling coffees in the world started out as the brainchild of an American salesman. He developed a method for making instant coffee. Rather than put his own name on his creation, he called it after the first hotel to stock his product, *Maxwell House*. His family name was, by the way, Cheek!

Fast and famous

A runaway success is *Nike* and small wonder, it is called after the Greek goddess of victory and who would argue with a woman?

Sing song

The founder's favourite song was the classic Al Jonson best seller "Sonny Boy" and Sonus is the Latin for sound and so Akio Morita called his company *Sony*. Another famous trade mark protected world-wide by registration!

Up and down

What goes up must come down, but not so visa versa unless that is, it's a *Yo-Yo*. This is probably one of the oldest toys used to frustrate and entertain mankind for centuries. Its origin is said to be found in ancient Greece where it was usually decorated with pictures of gods.

Big in the US of A

The Yo-Yo took off in the United States when a Philippine immigrant began producing them en masse in the 1900s. The word means "come back" in the native Filipino language.

Costly omission

The manufacturing rights were subsequently bought by an American who registered it as a trade mark. However, despite its huge initial success in that market, the registration must not have been maintained or policed because it has now become a generic term in that market.

Many owners

This assertion is supported as there is no other commonly used term to describe the toy. By contrast, in the Europe, despite the generic connotation, *Yo-Yo* is a registered trade mark owned by a variety of separate proprietors in different countries.

Registering smells as trade marks

In addition to names and symbols, slogans, colours, shapes and even smells can be exclusively yours by applying to register them as your particular trade mark. The variety that raises the most eyebrows is smells.

Tyres, darts, balls

Some examples of applications to date are; the smell of lavender in respect of automobile tyres by a Japanese manufacturer, the smell of stale beer for the flights on darts and tennis balls impregnated with the whiff of newly cut grass.

Success is in the air

A brand new wave of odours made their presence smelt in the marketplace. Some enterprises tested spraying the air of their establishments with a distinctive fragrance that they hoped would support brand awareness amongst their customers.

Tying it to shirts

That well known retailer of expensive shirts THOMAS PINK chose *air dried linen* as its olfactory mark and some stores in the United States were used to assess client reaction.

Flight of fancy

The first class and business class lounges in BRITISH AIRWAY'S locations at London and New York airports were sprayed with *meadow grass* so that the company's high flying clientele might experience a stronger brand awareness as they linger between flights.

Thinking outside the box

In an effort to capitalise on the ever- growing needs of the marketers, new forces are being called into play and companies are being formed to exploit the burgeoning demand.

Assailing the senses

There are now sensory design research laboratories emerging plus commercial interests who concentrate on meeting a variety of requirements.

Whiff it

Some of the marketing giants of soap powders and the like are interested in being able to get prospective users of their products to enjoy a whiff before purchase and appeal to the pocket through the nasal passages.

Scuff it

To this end a US point of sale company developed a method of applying advertising patches to the floor of supermarkets, which, when walked on, would cause to be emitted, the smell of an adjacently merchandised product.

Point of purchase

A wide selection of other marketers, from after-shave to coffee suppliers, examined the potential to highlight their offerings, where it matters, at point of purchase.

Oder prompt

Research was expanded into wider applications and the notion of having cash desk computer printers that can emit odours when, for instance they dispense a receipt. This marketing device could be used to prompt customers to purchase another product that is being promoted in store.

Sounds familiar

And then there are sound trade marks those that assist you to recognise brands by assaulting the ear. You may not realise it but there are many sounds in your daily life that you use to alert you to what's happening.

TV soap

For instance, you're in the kitchen and hear the signature music for your favourite TV soap programme coming from the adjacent room, so you rush into your living room to watch it.

High-brow cigars

J S Bach's "Air on a G string" has been registered as a trade mark by the manufacturers of HAMLET cigars.

Painted dogs

The sound of a certain dog barking was used to help identify, and brand, DULUX, that well known manufacturer of paint.

Rev it up

The unmistakable sound that comes from the exhaust of a HARLEY DAVIDSON was the subject of an application to have it registered as one of that company's exclusive trade marks.

HOW SOME MORE BEGAN

In this modern era many feel that it is the age of creativity when new ideas abound and poor old yesteryear had little going for it. This may be correct in some respects but it would be folly to overlook the huge strides that were made in the past and which, a great number of the great unwashed, unknowingly acknowledge in their daily lives. As we go about our business we use words and items which were in many respects "invented" by our forefathers.

Even in daily conversation we use expressions that find their origins in a logic that is long since past. "In the clink", a common enough phrase was first used in London decades ago and referred to someone being incarcerated in a prison which was sited on Clink Street. "Bedlam" a word used now to describe an unholy commotion taking place, was the name of a district in which a lunatic asylum was located.

Any others?

The writer would welcome some more examples of such words, particularly those with a commercial connection as instanced below. Readers may be surprised to learn that words like *hoarding* and *trolley* have interesting histories attaching to them.

Poster sites

Around 1850 a young man from the East End of London was quick to see the media potential presented by the introduction of new railways. He began renting from landlords' vacant sites along the lines for a few shillings. On these he erected advertising spaces which he in turn rented to advertisers at a considerable profit. The first users of these were manufacturers of patent medicines. The clever entrepreneur gave his name to the new medium, he was Samuel Hoarding.

Lit up

An advertising agent, Jacques Fonesque, back in the 1920s, discovered that a new product, NEON, which obviated the need for a filament, meant that the lighted tubing could be shaped into the form of letters. He was quick to exploit the potential and soon his signs were to be seen all over Paris. The first of these promoted *Cinzano*.

Off his trolley?

A Mr Goldman, the owner of a US chain of grocery shops was disappointed to realise that his customers invariably stopped shopping when their baskets got heavy. He enlisted the assistance of a handy man and between them came up with a contraption comprised of wheels attached to a folding chair and a basket where the seat should be. Shoppers ignored them until he got someone to wheel them around demonstrating their usefulness. And so, in 1930, the genesis of today's shopping trolley saw the light of day. Now, it too, carries advertising hoarding.

See-through technology

Many of the world's greatest inventions came about by chance. However, some level of expertise was required to bring some of them to successful fruition. Over one hundred years ago a German professor of physics, while working in his laboratory with a cathode-ray tube happened upon a new kind of radiation. This he realised could have novel uses. Wilhelm Roentgen christened his discovery "X-rays" and went on to develop them into a means of viewing the interior of the human body.

Negative side effects

This provided a great breakthrough for the medical profession. Unfortunately, it took some 50 years to realise that there was a downside to the innovation and that the procedure, like other forms of radiation, could cause cancer. On the other hand a bonus was that radiation could actually be used to good effect in the treatment of cancer by a technique known as radiotherapy.

Cat got your scan

This happened during the 1950s while the '60s saw the introduction of the CAT scan (or computerised axial tomography) which, using X-rays, scans the body in slices to produce a three dimensional picture of the various body parts.

Enter NRM

To avoid the negatives associated with radiation, the nuclear age spawned alternative diagnostic methodologies. By using powerful electromagnets it became possible to utilise nuclear magnetic resonance (NRM) imaging and record changes in the body's atoms. The NRM is then subjected to detailed analysis and can enable the production of three-dimensional images of internal organs.

Clear it and protect it

Of course, I cannot end without repeating myself again! If you intend to use a word, creative or otherwise, to trade mark your goods or services, at home or in export markets, make sure you do not infringe the rights of others.

Professional assistance

It is wise to use the skill of a trade mark attorney to make the necessary searches (particularly to uncover potentially *confusingly similar* rival marks) to clear the word for use in commerce. In addition apply to register it as a trade mark in your target markets and then, perhaps, your word will become as famous as so many others.

A PLAY ON WORDS

In this modern era many feel that it is the age of creativity when new ideas abound and poor old yesteryear had little going for it. This may be correct in some respects but it would be folly to overlook the huge strides that were made in the past and which, a great number of the great unwashed, unknowingly acknowledge in their daily lives.

Forefathers

As we go about our business we use words and items in sales and marketing which were in many respects "invented" by our forefathers.

Did you know?

Even in daily conversation we use expressions that find their origins in a logic that is long since past. "In the clink", a common enough phrase was first used in

London decades ago and referred to someone being incarcerated in a prison which was located on Clink Street.

Mad and skint

"Bedlam" a word used now to describe an unholy commotion taking place, was the name of a district in which a lunatic asylum was located. Skid Row is a street on a hill in Seattle, down which they used to slide timber to the docks from the plateau above. As a result it was a mucky street and not the most salubrious address in town. It was only fit for tramps and down and outs, hence the expression 'on skid row'.

Faux pas

The French call a fanlight un fasistas as a derivation of the German 'Was ist das?' (What is that?). Apparently this is what the German troops said as they pointed at these strange semi-circular shaped glass arrangements above doors, whilst they were invading France.

CONCLUSIONS: HOW ALL THIS HELPS YOU ACHIEVE YOUR OBJECTIVES

Conclusion

Devise/create/use

You now have a general overview of how to go about devising trade marks. You will, perhaps for the first time, appreciate the variety of forms they can take; symbols, logotypes, slogans, colours and so on.

Memorise

Each of them can be mobilised to attract attention, add interest, memorability and value to what you are offering. They are a variety of hooks that assist your potential, and existing, customers to instantly recognise your product or service.

The process

The thought process that I employ has been explained. The logic behind that which I shy away from and the route I take to achieve my aims are spelt out and supported by a wide variety of examples from disparate product/service categories.

You may follow my technique, a variation of it or devise your own methodology. It is not a precise science. But it is exciting, challenging and very rewarding when you strike gold!

Build your brand

You also know how to develop and utilise all of these in furtherance of building your branding whether that's for goods or services.

Home or abroad

In addition, you will now be familiar with the steps required to clear your brands for use and how to go about seeking to protect them. This can be for the domestic market or further afield.

Start or improve your business

From the myriad of stories and examples you now are familiar with the dangers that lurk out there. You are alert to the ways in which your business can be started or improved. You've seen how to invigorate existing businesses, find new angles for old business and how to dream up new lines.

Free publicity

Using all of this you have a road map to follow when it comes to increasing your profile and achieving free promotion and publicity.

Real life examples

What you have read is fully supported with a wide range of examples from real life experiences that illustrate each point. It has not been an academic lesson. It will save you time, money and heartache by showing you what to avoid and to exploit. You will benefit from knowing the direct route to creating a strong branding.

Know what's what

Misconceptions regarding the protection a company name affords you have been highlighted. Likewise, the misunderstanding that exclusivity comes with registration of a domain address. Both of these areas require your careful understanding of what they bestow upon you and what they do not!

Trade mark protection

Based on recognition of their limitations you will be well advised to look into registering your brands as trade marks, if they are suitable and available for such a process.

Other forms

We have referred to copyright in passing and to design registration. These are two areas that you could look into if you are so moved. They are not part of the remit of this book and are mentioned only as an aside.

Now you get started

It only remains now for you to take out that blank sheet of paper we referred to earlier and begin the task of working on your branding. It's not easy, it is time consuming but when you crack it, well worth it. **Enjoy**.